A-B-C, 1-2-3

A Teacher/Parent Resource
for
Teaching Beginning Concepts

by
Sue Goldsmith

for
Heidi and Katherine

ISBN 0-86530-024-0

TABLE OF CONTENTS

HOW TO USE THIS BOOK

As a early childhood teacher, you are the person students look to for learning and parents depend on for guidance. You are the person responsible for making certain that the all-important educational basics — numbers, letters, colors, etc. — are thoroughly understood by your students, and that these concepts are reinforced at home by their parents. **A-B-C, 1-2-3** has been written to help you do exactly that.

A-B-C, 1-2-3 meets the needs of both teachers and parents of early childhood students in the areas of the alphabet, colors, shapes, vowels and consonants, opposites and numbers. Each of these concepts is presented in a separate section, and each section is divided into two parts. The first part of each section includes detailed classroom activities and an annotated list of selected books. The second part of each section is a ready-to-reproduce "Take-Me-Home Learning Booklet," complete with a letter to parents, a list of activities for parents and children to do together, and an annotated reading list of excellent materials for parents and children to share.

The final section of the book is a series of annotated reading lists dealing with additional concepts of importance to the young learner. Here you will find books about days, months, seasons and special holidays. Be sure to make these books available to your students.

One other valuable aspect of this book is the following page entitled, "How To Help Your Child Be a Successful Student." Read it, reproduce it and send a copy home to each child's parents. It could make a big difference in the interest they take in their child's progress.

Keeping parents up-to-date on their child's progress and giving them a positive way to reinforce learning at home, shows parents that they have a major effect on their child's learning. **A-B-C, 1-2-3** helps teachers do this by providing excellent opportunities for keeping the channels of communication open.

HOW TO HELP YOUR CHILD BE A SUCCESSFUL STUDENT

Here are some important things you can do for your child. They do not take special skills, but they do take a little time. Give them a try, and you'll be pleased with the results.

Establish daily habits. Set up guidelines for a regular bedtime and a minimum number of hours of sleep each night. Emphasize the importance of regular attendance at school, and insist on it from the very beginning of your child's school career.

Praise your child. Be aware of what your child brings home. Applaud all good work done, and offer help in areas where it is needed.

Care for books. Treat the books and magazines in your home as prized possessions. Give them as gifts; make them treasures.

Talk to your child. Use a normal speaking voice, and include words your child does not know. Hearing new words will help your child learn them, which will make learning to read easier.

Listen to your child. Encourage your child to talk about all the things he or she sees and does. Ask questions to show that you are listening. This kind of exchange also helps a child learn new words.

Read to your child. This is the most important thing you can do. Read books to your child to show that reading is fun. Reading books yourself will show your child that you, too, enjoy reading. These actions will give your child the desire to learn to read.

Go to school. Children love to have their parents at school for open house and classroom visitation days. Show your child that you care about school by attending as many of these special events as possible.

Visit interesting places. Give your child lots of new experiences. Go to a zoo, a new building, a fair or to any interesting place or event in your area. Since children often like to read about things they have seen or done, take your child to the library and find books related to your experiences.

THE ALPHABET

THE ALPHABET

The alphabet is one of the first and most important concepts that children learn when they begin to talk. It is the foundation on which learning to read is based. This building process begins with letter recognition, then the attachment of a sound to a letter and then the combination of the sounds of several letters which make up a word.

Give your students every opportunity to develop the language, beginning reading, and sequencing skills that knowledge of the alphabet affords them.

Activities

• Give each student a booklet consisting of 13 sheets of paper with a construction paper cover. Direct students to write "My ABC Book" on the cover. Then have them write one capital and its matching lower-case letter on each page, beginning with "Aa." (Use the front and back of each sheet.) Each day, let students cut out pictures from magazines and newspapers, determine the beginning letter of each picture and paste the pictures on the appropriate pages of their alphabet books.

• Make a set of alphabet flashcards from 52 index cards. On each card, write either one capital or one lower-case letter. Then, spread the cards out face down on a table. Ask two students to participate, and explain that the object of the game is to match the lower-case letters with their capitals. Direct the first student to turn two cards face up. If these cards are a capital letter and its lower-case match, the student keeps that pair and turns up two more cards. If the cards do not match, the second student takes a turn. When all the cards have been matched, the student with more pairs wins the game.

11

- Fill a large pan with sand. Have a student practice writing letters in the sand. As each letter is written, the student should name it and tell what sound it makes.
- Give students practice in alphabet recognition. Write a row of capital letters on a sheet of paper in random order and ask a student to name the letters. Do the same with lower-case letters.

- Direct a student to form alphabet letters out of clay. (The student may make specific letters assigned by the teacher, or may make any letters he or she chooses.)
- Stencils are fun to use. Have students trace letters using stencils for practice in letter recognition and letter formation.
- Have each student make a letter on a piece of paper with glue. Provide macaroni or rice, and direct students to place these over the glue to form decorative letters. (Students can do the same activity using glitter.)
- Using a black marker, write either a capital or lower-case letter on a piece of burlap. Provide a large needle and thick thread. Ask a student to use the needle and thread to sew over the lines of the letter. (Make sure the students can manipulate the materials easily.)

- Give each student a page from a newspaper. Direct students to circle any given letter (example: s) each time it appears, and to draw a line under another given letter (example: w) each time it appears. This activity gives students practice in finding letters of the alphabet in printed words.
- Provide magazine and newspaper ads in which large letters are used. Give each student a piece of paper and some glue. Direct students to cut out letters from the ads and paste them on the paper in alphabetical order.

- Write three letters on a piece of paper and show them to a student. Ask the student to close his or her eyes and cover up one of the letters. Then ask the student to look again, and name the letter that has been covered. (As students improve at this game, increase the number of letters used.)
- Provide sandpaper, carpet samples and other different kinds of materials that students can cut. Direct students to trace (or draw) and cut out the letters of the alphabet from these materials. The different tactile sensations provided by these materials will delight the students and give them a new interest in the letters.
- Create an alphabet "twist" game. Divide a portion of an old sheet into 16 sections. Then choose eight letters, and write one capital or lower-case letter in each section. Make a spinner using the eight letters, and ask two students to volunteer to play. Direct the first student to spin, then to put one foot on the capital letter and the other foot on the lower-case letter. Direct the second student to follow the same pattern for his or her turn. Students continue to take turns stepping on letters until one falls and the other is declared the winner. (This game could be expanded to include the entire class by using a larger portion of a sheet and the entire alphabet.
- Make alphabet dominoes out of 26 index cards. Divide each card in half by drawing a line. On one side, write a capital letter; on the other side, write a different lower-case letter. Ask two students to play the game. Give half of the dominoes to each student. Direct one student to place any domino face up on the playing surface. The other student must play a domino that matches either side of the first domino (remember: capitals must be matched with lower-case letters), or that turn must be forfeited. Play continues until one player has used all his or her dominoes and is declared the winner.

Reading List

Allen, Joan. **The Happy Golden ABC.** Racine, WI: Golden Press, 1972.
    An ABC book of illustrations. Each letter is presented singly, and every item on the page that begins with that letter is labeled. (1-2)

Barton, Bryon. **Applebet Story.** New York: The Viking Press, 1973.
    A child follows an apple through the pages of the alphabet book. When the child gets to Z, the zebra eats it! (1-2)

Brown, Marcia. **All Butterflies: An ABC.** New York: Charles Scribner's Sons, 1974.
    An ABC book of animals to be read aloud. The interesting illustrations are done with an unusual artistic approach. (1-2)

Browning, Mary. **Apples, a Ball and Some Catnip.** Indianapolis, IN: E.C. Seale and Co., Inc., 1963.
    A nicely illustrated ABC book about cats, Muff, Buff and Fluff, and the trouble they cause. Part of the story is to be read by the teacher, and the other section is to be read by the children. (1-2)

Charles, Donald. **Shaggy Dog's Animal Alphabet.** Chicago: Children's Press, 1979.
    A clever alphabet book that is written in rhyme. (1-2)

Chess, Victoria. **Alfred's Alphabet Walk.** New York: Greenwillow Books, 1979.
> On Saturday morning, Alfred was to learn the letters from A to Z. He hid the alphabet book his mother gave him and went for a walk instead. But, by the time Alfred got home, he knew the letters because he saw all of them on his walk. (2)

Children's Television Workshop. **The Sesame Street Book of Letters.** New York: Little, Brown and Co., 1970.
> An unusual ABC picture book including alliterative poetry. The black-and-white drawings, with a few touches of color, and the out-of-sequence presentation of the letters make this book extremely interesting to children. (1-2)

Coletta, Irene and Hallie. **From A to Z.** Englewood Cliffs, NJ: Prentice-Hall, Inc., 1979.
> An ABC book using rebus sentences. Each page deals with a different letter. (2)

DeLage, Ida. **ABC Halloween Witch.** Champaign, IL: Garrard Publishing Co., 1977.
> This book tells a story about a witch as it introduces each letter of the alphabet. (K-2)

Delaunay, Sonia. **Sonia Delaunay's Alphabet.** New York: Thomas Y. Crowell, 1972.
> This book combines rhymes with very abstract presentations of the letters of the alphabet. (2)

Emberley, Ed. **Ed Emberley's ABC.** Boston: Little, Brown and Co., 1978.
> The proper formation of each letter of the alphabet is shown with step-by-step illustrations. (K-2)

Floyd, Lucy, and Lasky, Kathryn. **Agatha's Alphabet.** Chicago: Rand McNally and Co., 1975.
> This book is made up of beautifully illustrated two-page spreads for each letter of the alphabet. Each left-hand page presents a capital letter, and each right-hand page presents its lower-case form. Wonderful pictures accompany both forms of each letter. (P-2)

Friskey, Margaret. **Indian Two Feet and the ABC Moose Hunt.** Chicago: Children's Press, 1977.
> Indian Two Feet went on a moose hunt and took his arrows, his bow and his canoe. The alphabetical story continues in this manner to tell about all the things Indian Two Feet did while he was hunting. (K-2)

Fujikawa, Gyo. **Gyo Fujikawa's A to Z Picture Book.** New York: Grosset and Dunlap, 1974.
> Fantastic illustrations! Fujikawa has used black and white illustrations for a number of pictures and words that begin with a specific letter. Each black and white sequence is followed on the next page by a verse or a sentence about that letter with color illustrations. (P-2)

Garten, Jan. **The Alphabet Tale.** New York: Random House, 1964.
> The attractive illustrations and rhymes in this book lead the reader from one letter to the next. (1-2)

Gergely, Tibor. **Baby Wild Animals from A to Z.** New York: Golden Press, 1973.

An ABC picture book of wild baby animals. The capital and lower-case forms of each letter are reinforced with words and pictures. (K-2)

Gretz, Susanna. **Teddy Bears' ABC.** Chicago: Follett Publishing Co., 1974.

This book deals with teddy bears and the things they do from A to Z (dancing, eating, etc.). (K-2)

Gwynne, Fred. **Ick's ABC.** New York: Windmill Books, Inc., 1971.

A read-aloud ABC book with suggestions on what to do to keep our environment clean. (2)

Ladybird Books. **ABC.** London: Ladybird Books, no date.

A picture book of the alphabet. Nice illustrations for very young children. (P-1)

Manley, Deborah. **From A to Z.** Milwaukee, WI: Raintree Children's Books, 1979.

Describes and shows examples of each letter of the alphabet. This book is good for young children first learning the alphabet. (P-K)

Mayer, Mercer. **Little Monster's Alphabet Book.** New York: Golden Press, 1978.

Little Monster has an alphabet collection of things he likes to do, as well as a collection of things he likes to collect. (1-2)

Mendoza, George. **The Alphabet Boat.** New York: American Heritage Press, 1972.

This ABC book uses different parts of a boat to tell about each letter of the alphabet. (2-3)

Mendoza, George. **A Beastly Alphabet.** New York: Grosset and Dunlap, 1969.

Beastly looking animals, each depicting a letter of the alphabet, are being chased by one another. (2-3)

Mendoza, George. **The Christmas Tree Alphabet.** New York: The World Publishing Co., 1971.

Quotes from children around the world. Each child's quote stems from a different letter of the alphabet. (2)

Miles, Miska. **Apricot ABC.** Boston: Little, Brown and Co., 1969.

A story about an apricot tree and the animals that watch it grow. (2)

Newberry, Clare Turlay. **The Kittens' ABC.** New York: Harper and Row, 1965.

An ABC book of kittens, told in rhyme. (1-2)

Niland, Deborah. **ABC of Monsters.** New York: McGraw-Hill Book Co., 1976.

The monsters have a party, and do strange things from A (annoying apes) to Z (zigzagging all the way home). (1-2)

Oberman, Arline, and Oberman, Marvin. **The ABC of Living Things.** New York: Young Readers Press, Inc., 1972.

This nicely illustrated ABC book pictures living things on each page and includes a verse about each letter of the alphabet. (1-2)

Pease, Josephine. **ABC Book.** Chicago: Rand McNally and Co., no date.

An ABC book with rhyming phrases about each letter of the alphabet. (P-2)

Scarry, Richard. **Richard Scarry's ABC Word Book.** New York: Random House, 1971.
Little stories about the characters appear throughout the book. (1-2)

Scarry, Richard. **Richard Scarry's Things To Do.** New York: Golden Press. 1971.
Colors, shapes and sizes, parts of the body, months of the year, seasons, holidays and stories are illustrated in true Richard Scarry style. (1-2)

Seiden, Art. **My ABC Book.** New York: Wonder Books, 1974.
A basic ABC book filled with colorful pictures for very young children. (P-K)

Strejan, John. **The Alphabet Book.** Japan: Random House, no date.
A pop-up book of the ABC's illustrated with animals in the zoo. (1-2)

Tallon, Robert. **Zoophabets.** Indianapolis, IN: The Bobbs Merill Co., Inc., 1971.
An alphabet book of make-believe monsters. This book describes what each monster eats and where it lives. (2)

Tobias, Hosea, and Baskin, Leonard. **Hosie's Alphabet.** New York: The Viking Press. 1972.
Several different kinds of prints are combined with unusual types of animals to catch and hold the attention of either younger or older children (1-up)

Tudor, Tasha. **A Is for Annabelle.** Chicago: Rand McNally and Co., 1954.
An ABC book about Grandmother's doll and all the things that belong to the doll. (1-2)

Weigle, Oscar. **Fun with the Alphabet.** New York: Grosset and Dunlap, 1969.
An ABC book that can be used with preschoolers as well as older children. (P-3)

Weil, Lisl. **The Happy Ski ABC.** New York: G. P. Putnam's Sons, 1964.
An ABC book of skiing for children who want to learn about the sport. (3-up)

Wildsmith, Brian. **Brian Wildsmith's ABC.** New York: Oxford University Press, 1962.
A simple and endearing book with one picture on each page. All words are written in capital and lower-case letters. (K-1)

Williams, Garth. **The Big Golden Animal ABC.** Racine, WI: Western Publishing Co., 1957.
Capital and lower-case letters are presented on each page, along with a picture and the name of an appropriate animal. Children will really enjoy the large illustrations. (P-2)

Wing, Helen. **Happy Animal's ABC.** Chicago: Rand McNally and Co., 1956.
An ABC book for young children in which different animals depict each letter of the alphabet. (K-2)

Zacks, Irene. **Space Alphabet.** Englewood Cliffs, NJ: Prentice-Hall Inc., 1964.
The book connects each letter of the alphabet to a different piece of equipment used in space. (2)

Activities

1. Prepare some cookie dough, and choose a letter from the alphabet. Work with your child to make cookies in the capital and lower-case shapes of that letter. As you form the cookies, have your child tell you the sound the letter makes.

   After the cookies have baked and cooled, have a letter-tasting party. Ask your child to name different foods that begin with that letter. As you eat the cookies, discuss other words that begin with the letter you chose.

2. When you are traveling, play an alphabet game. Ask your child to watch the signs, and try to find all the letters of the alphabet in order, one to a sign (i.e.: on one sign, find an "A;" on the next sign, a "B," etc.). You may play this game as partners or as opponents, depending on your child's ability.

Take-Me-Home LEARNING BOOKLET

Dear Parents,

We have begun our study of the alphabet at school, and would like for you to reinforce this learning at home. Listed in this booklet are several fun and easy activities. Please share them with your child. Please books about the alphabet are to do them with your child in reviewing the alphabet letters and their sounds, you are helping your child learn to read. This is certainly spending "quality time" with your child!

Sincerely,

Fill in the missing letters of the alphabet.

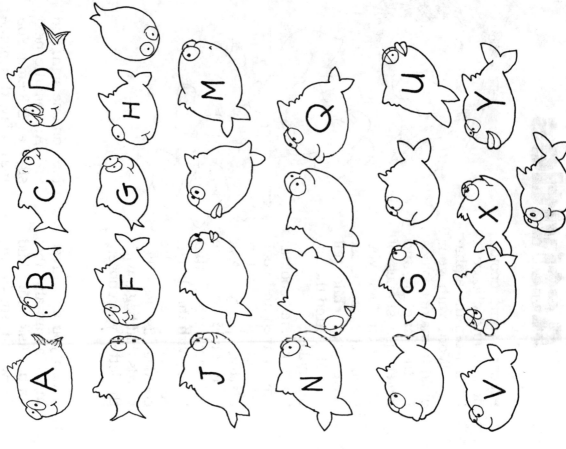

---

3. Pour out some alphabet cereal on the table. Have your child put the cereal in alphabetical order and then eat it.

4. Give your child some newspaper headlines or magazine ads (those that are printed in large letters), some paste and a sheet of paper. Ask your child to cut out one of each letter of the alphabet and paste them on the sheet of paper in alphabetical order.

5. Make some instant pudding and let your child "finger-paint" the letters of the alphabet on a tabletop, a sheet of waxed paper or a cabinet top. (Children always enjoy this activity because they get to lick their fingers!)

18

Reading List

Allen, Joan. **The Happy Golden ABC.** Racine, WI: Golden Press, 1972.
An ABC book of illustrations. Each letter is presented singly, and every item on the page that begins with that letter is labeled. (1-2)

Barton, Byron. **Applebet Story.** New York: The Viking Press, 1973.
A child follows an apple through the pages of the alphabet book. When the child gets to Z, the zebra eats it! (1-2)

Charles, Donald. **Shaggy Dog's Animal Alphabet.** Chicago: Children's Press. 1979.
A clever alphabet book that is written in rhyme. (1-2)

Emberley, Ed. **Ed Emberley's ABC.** Boston: Little, Brown and Co., 1978.
The proper formation of each letter of the alphabet is shown with step-by-step illustrations. (K-2)

Fujikawa, Gyo. **Gyo Fujikawa's A to Z Picture Book.** New York: Grosset and Dunlap, 1974.
Fantastic illustrations! Fujikawa has used black and white illustrations for a number of pictures and words that begin with a specific letter. Each black and white sequence is followed on the next page by a verse or a sentence about that letter with color illustrations. (P-2)

Manley, Deborah. **From A to Z.** Milwaukee, WI: Raintree Children's Books, 1979.
Describes and shows examples of each letter of the alphabet. This book is good for young children first learning the alphabet. (P-K)

Mayer, Mercer. **Little Monster's Alphabet Book.** New York: Golden Press, 1978.
Little Monster has an alphabet collection of things he likes to do, as well as a collection of things he likes to collect. (1-2)

Niland, Deborah. **ABC of Monsters.** New York: McGraw-Hill Book Co., 1976.
The monsters have a party and they do strange things from A (annoying apes) to Z (zigzagging all the way home). (1-2)

Strejan, John. **The Alphabet Book.** Japan: Random House, no date.
A pop-up book of the ABC's illustrated with animals in the zoo. (1-2)

Wildsmith, Brian. **Brian Wildsmith's ABC.** New York: Oxford University Press, 1962.
A very simple and endearing book with one picture on each page. All words are written in capital and lower-case letters. (K-1)

Zacks, Irene. **Space Alphabet.** Englewood Cliffs, NJ: Prentice-Hall, Inc., 1964.
The book connects each letter of the alphabet to a different piece of equipment used in space. (2)

COLORS

COLORS

In the primary grades, students work with colors and color words almost every single day. Knowledge of the colors red, blue, green, yellow, orange, black, brown, purple, pink and white is an essential part of learning.

Students need to be able to recognize and discriminate between colors and to identify color words when written, for many reasons. Colors are frequently prominent on warning signs and labels. Matching and combining colors can make getting dressed more interesting to students. The ability to discriminate between colors is an integral part of developing hand coordination during color exercises in the classroom.

Activities

- Gather several colored blocks or colored pieces of paper. Ask a student to point out all the red shapes, then all the blue shapes, and so on. (This activity is good for color and/or shape recognition.)
- Provide a strong piece of cord and beads of different colors. Ask a student to find and string together all beads of one color. Continue the activity with beads of another color until all colors have been strung together.

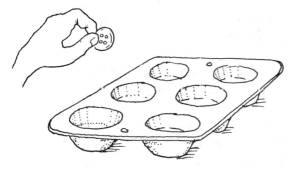

- Collect several buttons of different colors and give them to a student along with a cupcake pan. Label each section of the pan with a different color and ask the student to sort the buttons into the appropriate sections.

- Make a set of color flashcards. Provide two cards for every color used. On one card, write the name of the color; on the other card, use the color itself. Spread all cards face down on the playing surface, and ask two students to play "Color Match." The first student turns two cards face up. If the cards are a match (i.e.: color word and color), that student keeps that pair and continues to play. If the cards do not match, they are turned face down and the second student takes a turn. The student with more pairs at the end of the game wins.

- Play "Color Watch." Divide the class into two teams. Ask the first team to look around the room and name all the red things. Give a point for each correct answer. When the first team has finished, ask the opposing team if it can add to the first team's answers. If so, give a point for each new answer. Then ask the opposing team to find and name all the blue things in the room. Continue the game in this manner as long as students are interested.

- Supply students with watercolors, brushes and paper. Direct each student to make a color booklet by painting yellow things on one page, purple things on another page, etc. After the paint has dried, ask students to write the correct color word on each page. Then staple the pages together, and let each student keep his or her booklet for reference.

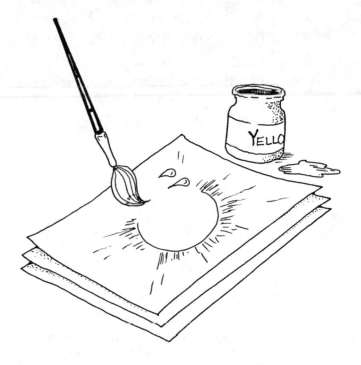

Reading List

Allington, Richard L. **Beginning To Learn About Colors.** Milwaukee, WI: Raintree Children's Books, 1979.
Good for learning about colors, and how to mix them to make new colors. (K-2)

Color. New York: Grosset and Dunlap, 1973.
This color book shows different ways that colors are used in everyday life. Traffic lights are red, yellow and green; berries are bright colors and paints can be mixed together to make many different colors. (1-2)

Crews, Donald. **Freight Train.** New York: Greenwillow Books, 1978.
A train that has different colored cars goes through tunnels and zooms by cities. (1-2)

Emberley, Ed. **Green Says Go.** Boston: Little Brown and Co., 1968.
This book explains the primary and secondary colors and tells how to mix the colors to form new ones. The author also explains how different colors may mean different things in different situations. (2)

Hoban, Tanya. **Is It Red? Is It Yellow? Is It Blue?** New York: Green-willow Books, 1978.

This picture book, depicting color in everyday life, is an adventure in color. (P-2)

Hoffman, Beth. **Red Is for Apples.** New York: Random House, 1966.

A nicely illustrated book of colors and rhymes. (1-2)

Howard, Katherine, and Miller, J.P. **Do You Know Your Colors?** New York: Random House, 1978.

The author uses each color in different situations so children can see the many different ways colors may be used. (1-2)

Max, Peter. **The Peter Max Land of Yellow.** New York: Franklin Watts, 1970.

A book of colors that tells a story about a king and queen. (2)

Pienkowski, Jan. **Colors.** New York: Harvey House, 1975.

On each left-hand page is a color and its color word, and on each facing page is a picture of something that color. (1-2)

Radlauer, Ruth, and Radlauer, Ed. **Colors.** Los Angeles: Bowmar Publishing Corp., 1968.

What things are red? The author talks about each color in this way and then shows samples of each color. The author then asks who is wearing that color. (1-2)

Ricketts, Ann, and Ricketts, Michael. **Color.** New York: Grosset and Dunlap, 1973.

This book depicts colors in different settings, and shows how colors are used to tell us things (i.e.: red means danger; yellow means warning, etc.). There is an activity to do at the end of the book. (1-2)

Stein, Sara. **A Piece of Red Paper.** Englewood Cliffs, NJ: Small World Enterprises, Inc., 1973.

A combination color and shape book done in abstract designs. (1-2)

Wingfield, Ethel. **Colours.** Loughborough, England: Ladybird Books, no date.

Which things are red? Which things are blue? These are some of the questions asked in this color book. (1-2)

Activities

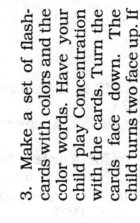

1. You need a piece of heavy string and some beads of different colors. Have your child string the beads of one color together. Then, decide on the next color and ask your child to string those beads together.

2. Have your child sort buttons according to colors into a cupcake pan. All the reds go together, all the blues go together, all the greens together.

3. Make a set of flashcards with colors and the color words. Have your child play Concentration with the cards. Turn the cards face down. The child turns two face up. If they match, the child keeps that pair. If they do not match, then he or she must turn them back over.

4. Ask your child to name the color of each article of clothing he or she puts on while dressing. Or, do the same activity when your child is getting ready for bed.

Take-Me-Home LEARNING BOOKLET

Dear Parents,

We have begun our study of colors at school. Your child needs to be able to recognize the colors and be able to know the words that stand for them.

Included in this booklet are different colors that you can use activities about colors. You will also find a reading list to guide you as share with your child. You as activities your child. at your local library. Use these materials to you look for books on colors to reinforce the ideas and help concepts we have been learning at school. This will be a "colorful" way to spend time with your child.

Sincerely,

26

Reading List

Allington, Richard L. **Beginning To Learn About Colors.** Milwaukee, WI: Raintree Children's Books, 1979.
Good for learning about colors and how to mix them to make different colors. (1-2)

Color. New York: Grosset and Dunlap, 1976.
A color book of activities for children to do. (1-2)

Crews, Donald. **Freight Train.** New York: Greenwillow Books, 1978.
A train that has different colored cards goes through tunnels and zooms by cities. (1-2)

Hoban, Tanya. **Is It Red? Is It Yellow? Is It Blue?** New York: Greenwillow Books, 1978.
This picture book, depicting color in everyday life, is an adventure in color.

Howard, Katherine, and Miller, J.P. **Do You Know Your Colors?** New York: Random House, 1978.
The author uses each color in different situations so the children can see the many different ways colors may be used. (1-2)

Max, Peter. **The Peter Max Land of Yellow.** New York: Franklin Watts, Inc., 1970.
A book about a king and queen and how they use colors. (2)

Pienkowski, Jan. **Colors.** New York: Harvey House, 1975.
Each two-page spread in this book presents a color and its name on the left, and a picture of something that color on the right. (1-2)

Ricketts, Ann, and Ricketts, Michael. **Color.** New York: Grosset and Dunlap, 1973.
This color book depicts colors in different settings and shows how colors are used to convey meanings (for example, red means danger; yellow means warning, etc.). There is an activity to do at the end of the book. (1-2)

Stein, Sara. **A Piece of Red Paper.** Englewood Cliffs, NJ: Small World Enterprises Inc., 1973.
A combination color and shape book done in abstract designs. (1-2)

Wingfield, Ethel. **Colours.** Loughborough, England: Ladybird Books, no date.
Which things are red? Which things are blue? These are examples of some of the questions in this color book. (1-2)

SHAPES

SHAPES

The study of shapes in the primary grades is emphasized both in math and in reading. The four basic shapes — the square, the circle, the triangle and the rectangle — are the ones most frequently investigated. Since these shapes are the most common to our world, they are consequently the ones that young students need to learn first.

To add extra excitement to the study of shapes, link this information to the world outside the classroom. Children quickly become aware of the shapes around them (i.e.: circles on traffic signals, rectangular street signs, triangular caution signs, etc.), and this linkage will make them more interested in excelling at shape formation and discrimination.

Activities

- Provide a student with a set of colored blocks or shapes cut out of colored paper. Ask the student to show you all the new shapes he or she can make by combining the blocks or shapes.
- Ask each student to draw and cut out several squares, triangles, circles and rectangles. Then, direct each student to construct a person out of the shapes he or she has produced.

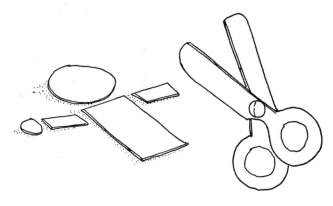

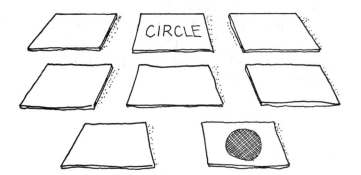

- Make a set of "shape" flashcards out of eight index cards. Write one shape name on each of four cards, and draw one shape on each of the four remaining cards. Place the cards face down on the playing surface, and ask a student to turn up two cards at a time. If the two cards match, the student keeps the pair; if not, the student must turn the two cards face down and try again.

• To increase the number of cards, incorporate color into the previous game. Add pairs of cards which are keyed to each other not only by shape, but also by color (i.e.: a card which has the word "square" written on it in green could only match the card on which a green square has been drawn). These additions will make the game more difficult, and will also make the deck large enough so that two or more students can play together.

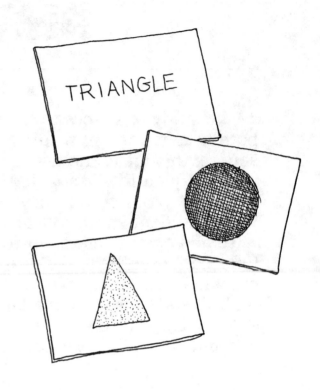

• Provide beads of different shapes, and ask a student to string several of them together. Then, give the student a piece of paper, and ask him or her to copy on paper the pattern made by stringing the beads.

• Culminate the study of shapes by making a "Shapes Booklet." On Monday, assign a shape for students to search for that night. On Tuesday, ask students to label a sheet of paper with the shape name, and draw on the paper whatever objects they saw the night before that contained that shape. Then assign a shape for Tuesday night, and continue in this manner for the rest of the week. By the end of Friday, the booklets will have been completed, and each student will have a "Shapes" reference book to keep. (Note: This activity could also be done as a class project. In this case, all shapes would be drawn in one large booklet, and the completed project would become a classroom reference book.)

Reading List

Allington, Richard L. **Beginning To Learn About Shapes.** Milwaukee, WI: Raintree Children's Books, 1979.
This book presents pictures with different shapes in them. (For example, a picture of a monkey has circles for eyes.) The book covers the following shapes: circle, square, triangle, rectangle, star, oval, pentagon, hexagon, heptagon and octagon. (1-2)

Budney, Blossom. **A Kiss Is Round.** New York: Lothrop, Lee and Shepard Co., 1954.
A book about circles. The author describes many different things that are in the shape of a circle. (1-2)

Carle, Eric. **My Very First Book of Shapes.** New York: Thomas Y. Crowell, 1974.
Each page of this book pictures shapes on the top half and illustrations on the bottom half which are to be matched. (P-1)

Children's Television Workshop. **The Sesame Street Book of Shapes.** Boston: Little, Brown and Co., 1970.
Circles, squares, rectangles and triangles are discussed in this book. The author asks the reader to choose items from the page that match these shapes. (1-2)

Hoban, Tana. **Circles, Triangles and Squares.** New York: Macmillan Pub. Co., 1974.
The use of black-and-white photography in this book emphasizes the different shapes to be found within the pictures, including everything from the circles in a little girl's glasses to the squares in a rabbit's cage. (K-2)

Reiss, John J. **Shapes.** New York: Bradbury Press Inc., 1974.
Circles, squares and triangles are the subject of this book. There are lots of examples of each shape throughout its pages. (1-2)

Schlein, Miriam. **Shapes.** New York: William Scott, Inc., no date.
The book describes circles and squares in a rhyming story. (1-2)

Thoburn, Tina. **Discovering Shapes.** New York: Western Publishing Co., 1970.
Everything has a shape. In this book, the author finds things that have similar shapes. The author has also listed activities to do. (1-2)

Wingfield, Ethel. **Shapes.** Loughborough, England: Ladybird Books, no date.
This book gives samples of what different things shapes can become. (For example, sails on a sailboat are triangles.) (1-2)

Activities

1. Ask your child to draw, color and cut out several different squares, circles, triangles and rectangles. Let your child play with these shapes and put them together in many different ways. When your child has put together a picture that he or she would like to keep, provide paste and some paper, and help your child glue the creation in place.

2. Ask your child to look around the room and notice some of the shapes that make up the things in the room. Then, name a shape, and ask your child to show you all the things in the room that have that shape. (This is also a good travel activity.)

Take-Me-Home LEARNING BOOKLET

Dear Parents,
The world is filled with many shapes, and right now, your child is learning about some of them. We are studying the circle, the square, the triangle — the rectangle and the triangle — but also the most important ones.
Included in this booklet are some activities and books about shapes that you and your child can share. Please help your child excel in school by doing these things and reading these books together at home.
Sincerely,

34

Carle, Eric. **My Very First Book of Shapes.** New York: Thomas Y. Crowell, 1974. Each page of this book pictures shapes on the top half and illustrations on the bottom half which are to be matched. (P-1)

Children's Television Workshop. **The Sesame Street Book of Shapes.** Boston: Little, Brown and Co., 1970. Circles, squares, rectangles and triangles are discussed in this book. The author asks the reader to choose items from the page that match these shapes. (1-2)

Hoban, Tana. **Circles, Triangles and Squares.** New York: Macmillan Pub. Co. 1974. The use of black-and-white photography in this book emphasizes the different shapes to be found within the pictures, including everything from the circles in a little girl's glasses to the squares in a rabbit's cage. (K-2)

Reiss, John J. **Shapes.** New York: Bradbury Press Inc., 1974. Circles, squares and triangles are the subject of this book. There are lots of examples of each shape throughout its pages. (1-2)

Schlein, Miriam. **Shapes.** New York: William Scott, Inc., no date. This book describes circles and squares in a rhyming story. (1-2)

Thoburn, Tina. **Discovering Shapes.** New York: Western Publishing Co., 1970. Everything has a shape. In this book, the author finds things that have similar shapes. There are also activities to do. (1-2)

3. Challenge your child to draw something (a person, a tree, a building, etc.) using only one shape. (For example, if your child wanted to use triangles to make a person, he or she could use lots of triangles, but no squares, rectangles or circles.) Let your child make at least one picture using each shape, and write the name of the shape used on each picture.

4. Do some silly exercises with your child. Name a shape, and then both of you try to make your bodies into that shape. If you can't make a shape with your whole body, use just your arms, legs or hands.

Reading List

Allington, Richard L. **Beginning To Learn About Shapes.** Milwaukee, WI: Raintree Children's Books, 1979. This book about all kinds of shapes presents pictures with the different shapes in them. (For example, a picture of a monkey has circles for eyes.) The book covers the following shapes: circle, square, triangle, rectangle, star, oval, pentagon, hexagon, heptagon and octagon. (1-2)

Budney, Blossom. **A Kiss Is Round.** New York: Lothrop, Lee and Shepard Co., 1954. A book about circles. The author describes many different things that are in the shape of a circle. (1-2)

VOWELS and CONSONANTS

VOWELS and CONSONANTS

The knowledge of vowel and consonant sounds is essential to the process of learning to read. Students must first learn the various sounds each vowel or consonant can make, and then must develop the ability to figure out which sounds the letters stand for within a given word. To aid students in this process, teach the following rules:

1. When two vowels are together in a word, the first one makes a long sound and the second one is silent. (example: read)

2. If there is only one vowel in a word and it is followed by a consonant, the vowel sound is short. (example: can)

3. When a word has an "e" at the end and there is a v-c-e (vowel-consonant-e) pattern, the first vowel makes a long sound and the "e" is silent. (example: make)

4. When a vowel is the last letter of a word, it makes a long sound. (example: we)

Of course, the English language is such that these guidelines do not always apply. Usually, however, they do apply, and will certainly be of great help to a student just learning to read.

Activities

• Make a "Consonant Box." Find several objects which have names that start with consonants. Place these in a box, and ask a student to work with you. Pull out one object at a time from the box, and ask the student to tell you the beginning letter and sound of the object's name. (This same activity can be done with vowels, too.)

- Play "Consonant Trip" with just a few students or the entire class. Begin the game by saying, "I am going on a trip, and I'm going to take a_____ ." (Fill in the blank with a word that begins with the consonant of your choice; for example: "I am going on a trip, and I'm going to take a suitcase.") A student then repeats the sentence and adds another item with the same beginning consonant. ("I am going on a trip, and I'm going to take a suitcase and some socks.") Play continues in this manner until each student has contributed, or until the teacher stops the game and introduces a different consonant. (If a student cannot repeat the sentence with the additions in order, the student must forfeit that turn.

  Vary this game by using words that start with vowels, or by using words that contain short or long vowel sounds in them.

- Ask a student to listen as you say a word (or watch as you show a picture). Then, tell the student to write the beginning sound of that word on a piece of paper or a chalkboard. Continue this activity for as long as you wish. (This can also be a whole-class activity.)

- Using the proper markings, write the short vowels along one side of a piece of paper. Write the long vowels along the other side. Give a student the paper and a clothespin. Ask the student to listen as you say a word (or show a picture card), and then have him or her clip the clothespin over the correct vowel sound in the word.

- Reinforce a student's ability to hear vowel sounds by using rhyming words. Ask the student to list all the rhyming words he or she can think of that have a given vowel sound. (This can also be a whole-class activity.)

- Divide a heavy sheet of paper into four sections. In each section, print one of the vowel pronunciation rules given on the first page of this section. Then, make a set of cards, each bearing a word (and/or a picture) that fits one of the rules. Give these materials to a student, and direct him or her to sort the cards into the correct sections.

- Provide some clay, and instruct a student to form a given consonant. Let the student use the rest of the clay to make various things which have names beginning with that sound.

Berenstain, Stan, and Berenstain, Jan. **The B Book.** New York: Random House, 1971.

Silly riddles of "b" words in the Berenstains' usual style. (1-2)

Berenstain, Stan, and Berenstain, Jan. **C Is for Clown.** New York: Random House, 1972.

A book of "c" words used by Clarence the Clown, with humorous illustrations. (1-2)

The Sounds Book. Newark, NJ: Britannica Discovery Library, 1974.

A book about different sounds that are made by animals, machines, etc. (1-2)

Chardiet, Bernice. **C Is for Circus.** New York: Walker and Co., 1971.

This beginning sounds book about a circus includes monkey shows, elephants and clowns. (K-2)

Hayward, Linda. **Letters, Sounds, and Words: A Phonics Dictionary.** New York: Platt and Munk, Publishers, 1973.

A very helpful dictionary of beginning sounds, blends and vowels. (2)

Moncure, Jane Belk. **My "D" Sound Box.** Chicago: The Child's World, Inc., 1978.

Little d collected "d" things for her sound box. She found lots of different dolls and started making lots of "d" things for them (doll clothes, dogs, ducks, a dollhouse). At the end of the book, the child can read the words with Little d. (1-2)

Moncure, Jane Belk. **My "R" Sound Box.** Chicago: The Child's World, Inc., 1978.

This book is about the sound that the letter "r" makes. The author tells the story about Little r and how she thinks of words that begin with that letter. Pleasant story and pictures. (1-2)

Moncure, Jane Belk. **My "V" Sound Box.** Chicago: The Child's World, Inc., 1979.

This book contains the sound of "v." The author illustrates and tells the story of a little girl, v. She has a box where she puts "v" things. A story with words that a first or second grader can read. (1-2)

Moncure, Jane Belk. **Short A and Long A Play a Game.** Chicago: The Child's World, Inc., 1979.

Long a and Short a race to find things that begin with their names. Then they race to find things that contain their sounds in the middle. The reader must discover which vowel wins the race. There is an activity page for children. (1-2)

Stanek, Muriel. **Growl When You Say R.** Chicago: Albert Whitman and Co., 1979.

Robbie moves to a new school. The children make fun of him because he has a speech problem. Robbie's teacher puts him into a speech class. The story deals with the emotional upheaval of a child who has a speech problem and how it is dealt with in school. (1-2)

Activities

1. Using alphabet cereal, place the letters A-Z in a row. Ask your child to tell you something that begins with each sound. Every time your child is correct, let him or her eat that letter and then go on to the next one.

2. Take your child to the grocery store with you. As you go up and down the aisles, ask your child to look for items beginning with a certain sound.

3. To help your child recognize different vowel sounds, play a rhyming word game. Say a word, then ask your child to tell you what vowel sound is being used. Then, tell your child to say a word that rhymes with your word. Work with one sound for a while, and then switch to another.

4. Point out different articles of furniture and clothing in your home, and ask your child to say the beginning sound, the vowel sound and the ending sound of each word.

Take-Me-Home LEARNING BOOKLET

Dear Parents,

Right now, your child is learning to read by listening to the sounds within words and relating these sounds to the letters of the alphabet. Knowing the sounds made by the vowels and consonants makes it easier for your child to sound out new words and recognize familiar ones.

Working with your child to practice these vowels and consonant sounds at home can be a fun and rewarding experience. Look in this booklet to find some activities and books you and your child can share. You will both be glad you did.

Sincerely,

Reading List

Berenstain, Stan, and Berenstain, Jan. **C Is for Clown.** New York: Random House, 1972.
A book of "c" words used by Clarence the Clown. Funny illustrations. (1-2)

Chardiet, Bernice. **C Is for Circus.** New York: Walker and Co., 1971.
This beginning sounds book about a circus includes monkey shows, elephants and clowns. (K-2)

Moncure, Jane Belk. **My "D" Sound Box.** Chicago: The Child's World, Inc., 1978.
Little d collected "d" things for her sound box. She found lots of different dolls and started making lots of "d" things for them (doll clothes, dogs, ducks, a dollhouse). At the end of the book, the child can read the words with Little d. (1-2)

Moncure, Jane Belk. **My "L" Sound Box.** Chicago: The Child's World, Inc., 1978.
Little l had a box of things that began with "l." Everything Little l found that began with this letter was put into his "l" box. At the end of the book, the child can read the list of things Little l found. (1-2)

Moncure, Jane Belk. **Short A and Long A Play a Game.** Chicago: The Child's World, Inc., 1979.
Long a and Short a race to find things that begin with their names. Then they race to find things that contain their sounds in the middle. An activity page for children is included. (1-2)

Moncure, Jane Belk. **Short E and Long E Play a Game.** Chicago: The Child's World, Inc., 1979.
Same format as previous page. (1-2)

Moncure, Jane Belk. **Short I and Long I Play a Game.** Chicago: The Child's World, Inc., 1979.
Same format as previous page. (1-2)

Moncure, Jane Belk. **Short O and Long O Play a Game.** Chicago: The Child's World, Inc., 1979.
Same format as previous page. (1-2)

Moncure, Jane Belk. **Short U and Long U Play a Game.** Chicago: The Child's World, Inc., 1979.
Same format as previous page. (1-2)

Stanek, Muriel. **Growl When You Say R.** Chicago: Albert Whitman and Co., 1979.
Robbie moves to a new school. The children make fun of him because he has a speech problem. Robbie's teacher puts him into a speech class. This story shows the emotional upheaval of a child that has a speech problem. (1-2)

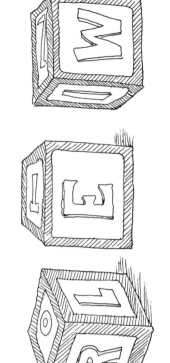

OPPOSITES

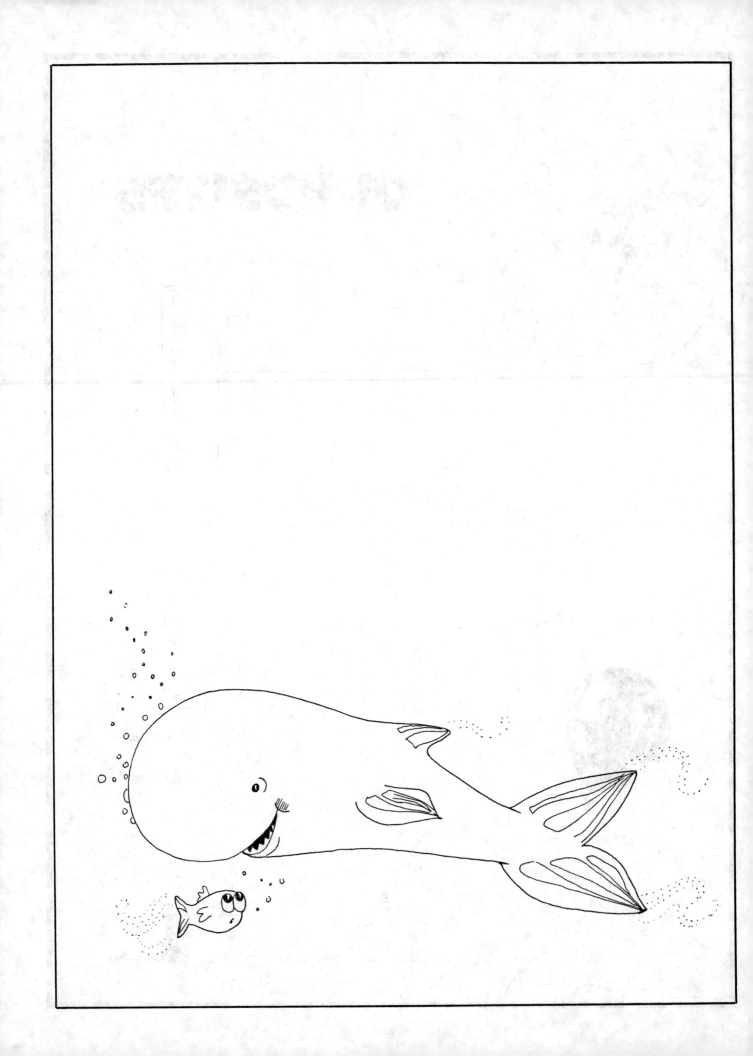

OPPOSITES

An understanding of the concept of opposites is very important to primary students. Many sets of opposites are directional words — up/down, left/right, top/bottom, above/below, before/after and under/over. Teachers must make certain that students can define opposite words, and can distinguish between them.

The study of opposites can be very exciting to students. Once the concept of opposites is grasped, students will look enthusiastically for new applications of this concept wherever they go. Take advantage of this excitement by encouraging students to report any new sets of opposites they discover, and by discussing these new examples with the entire class.

Activities

- Make a set of specific instructions for students to follow in drawing a picture (for example: "Draw a circle on the right side of your paper for the sun; draw a bird at the top of your paper, draw some grass at the bottom of the paper; draw a nest under the bird," etc.). Post the instructions where all students can see them, and ask students to follow the directions carefully.

- Turn the above activity around! Let each student draw his or her own picture. Then sit with one student at a time, and let him or her tell you about the picture (for example: "I put a tree to the left of the house. I drew a mermaid under the ocean").

- Provide six sets of objects that are alike except for size (for example: use cereal boxes, tin cans, pencils, etc.). Line these up in random order, and ask a student to match the objects which are alike.

- Play "Opposite Match." Make a list of about 20 words and their opposites, and write only one word on a card. Turn all the cards face down on the playing surface and ask two students to take turns trying to match words with their opposites. The student who has matched more pairs by the end of the game is the winner.

- As a class project, make an "Opposites Book." Ask students to name all the opposite sets they can think of. Print each set on its own page. Give each page to a different student volunteer for illustration. Bind the finished pages into a booklet, and add a student-illustrated cover. Add the booklet to your classroom reference library.

- Make a set of "Opposite Dominoes" using index cards and the list of opposites from the above activity. Divide each card in half with a line, and write a word in each section. (Be sure to write each word in a pair on a different card!) Ask two students to play the game just as regular dominoes are played, except they must match up opposites. The first student to match up all his or her dominoes wins the game.

- Play "Simon Says" using left and right directions (for example: "Put your left foot up; put your right hand on your nose; put your left foot behind your right one; put your right hand above your head").

- Have a class discussion about "alike and different." You will need pictures of items within a category to make your point. For instance, when you discuss vegetables, you will need pictures of different vegetables. You can then point to the pictures and explain that all these items are alike because they are vegetables, but that they are also different because there are different kinds of vegetables (or cars or animals, etc.).

Allington, Richard L. **Beginning To Learn About Opposites.** Milwaukee, WI: Raintree Children's Books, 1979.
In this book of opposites, these concept words are illustrated: big/little, same/different, young/old, top/bottom, strong/weak, many/few, front/back, tall/short, alive/dead, left/right, high/low, before/after, far/near and over/under. (1-2)

Berenstain, Stan, and Berenstain, Jan. **Inside, Outside, Upside Down.** New York: Random House, 1968.
Little Bear is inside a box, outside a box and then upside down all the way to town. Good for learning what inside, outside and upside down mean. (K-2)

Berg, Jean. **Big Bug, Little Bug.** New York: Follett Pub. Co., 1964.
All about a bug who meets other creatures that are bigger than he. He finally meets someone that is smaller (an ant), and they become friends. (1-2)

Berkley, Ethel. **Big and Little, Up and Down.** New York: Young Scott Books, no date.
This book compares things that are big and little and gives several examples of these concepts. The author compares these opposites also: high/low, top/bottom, wide/narrow, tall/short and under/over. (1-2)

Berkley, Ethel **The Size of It and Ups and Downs.** Chippewa Falls, WI: E.M. Hale and Co., no date.
The first section of this book introduces the following concepts and then compares them: big, little, long, tall, wide, narrow and short. The second section of the book introduces each of these concept words with questions and illustrations: up, down, high, top, bottom, low, under, over. (1-2)

Blair, Mary. **The Up and Down Book.** New York: Golden Press, 1964.
A book about things that go up and things that go down. (1-2)

Eastman, P.D. **Big Dog . . . Little Dog: A Bedtime Story.** New York: Random House, 1973.
A big dog, Fred, and his little dog friend, Ted, like to do the opposite of each other. One likes to ski; one likes to skate. One likes to drive slowly, and the other likes to drive fast. A good story for learning about opposites. (1-2)

Elwart, Joan Potter. **In, On, Under and Through.** Racine, WI: Whitman Publishing Co., no date.
A child looks on, in, under and through things in this story. Excellent for introducing these concept words. (1-2)

Goldin, Augusta. **The Bottom of the Sea.** New York: Thomas Y. Crowell Co., 1966.
This is a "Let's Read and Find Out Science Book" about the ocean and all the things you will find on its floor. (2-6)

Hann, Jacquie. **Up Day, Down Day.** New York: Four Winds Press, 1978.
A little boy and his friend go fishing together. One of the children catches a cold and must stay home, while the other one has to go to school. Attractive illustrations. (1-2)

Hayward, Linda. **Going Up! The Elevator Counting Book.** New York: Golden Press, 1980.

Grover takes all the Muppets for a ride on the elevator. They go up to the top floor of the hotel to swim. When the swimming pool closes, they go down. (1-2)

Hoban, Tana. **Over, Under and Through.** New York: The Macmillan Co., 1973.

This is a picture book of these concept words: over, under, through, on, in, around, across, between, beside, below, against, behind. Good illustrations. (P-2)

Hughes, Shirley. **Up and Up.** Englewood Cliffs, NJ: Prentice-Hall Inc., 1979.

A picture book about a little girl who eats a very large Easter egg. She is so full that she floats around the sky. Her family tries to get her down using several different methods. (1-2)

Hulbert, Elizabeth. **Out and In.** New York: Scholastic Book Service, 1970.

The concept words in, out, up, down, under and around are used while telling a story about a little boy who wanted to go somewhere. (1-2)

Jardine, Maggie. **Up and Down.** New York: Wonder Books, 1965.

A book about up and down. A good book for first and second graders to read. (1-2)

Jaynes, Ruth. **The Biggest House.** Los Angeles: Bowmar Pub. Corp., 1968.

The "biggest house" is an apartment building where a little boy, Robert, lives with his family. The biggest house has many doors and windows,and many people live in the house. This book not only gives children an idea of what big means, but they also learn what an apartment building is. (1-2)

Kingsley, Emily Perl. **Big Bird and Little Bird's Big and Little Book.** New York: Western Publishing Co., Inc., 1977.

Big Bird likes big things and Little Bird likes little things. They also like to do things that are the opposite of each other. (1-2)

Lund, Doris. **I Wonder What's Under.** New York: Parents Magazine Press, 1970.

Dudley wonders what's under his bed and keeps his father up until he tells him. This is a good bedtime story for young children. (1-2)

Manley, Deborah. **The Other Side.** Milwaukee, WI: Raintree Children's Books, 1979.

This book is a basic introduction of the opposites fast and slow, top and bottom, tall and short, clean and dirty, happy and sad, front and back, full and empty, big and small, long and short and thin and fat. (1-2)

Miller, J.P. **Big and Little.** New York: Random House, 1976.

A cute picture book of these opposite words: tall, short, fat, thin, few, many, over, under, up, down, in and out. (P-2)

Murdock, Hy. **Big and Little.** Loughborough, England: Ladybird Books, no date.

This book is about the concept words big, little, large, small, thin, fat, short, tall, long, up, down, high, low, on, off, out, in, over and under. The book contains good illustrations of each. (1-2)

Opposite Set. **Big and Little** New York: Grosset and Dunlap, 1977.

This book is about the opposites big and little. It shows many examples of these concept words. The end of the book has two art ideas and a game that deals with these concepts. (1-2)

Opposite Set. **Fast and Slow.** New York: Grosset and Dunlap, 1977.

A picture book about the opposites fast and slow. (1-2)

Opposite Set. **Front and Back.** New York: Grosset and Dunlap, 1977.

A good book for introduction of the concepts front and back. There are many examples of each of these concepts, along with activities in the back of the book. (1-2)

Opposite Set. **Noisy and Quiet.** New York: Grosset and Dunlap, 1977.

This is a book about the opposites noisy and quiet. Great illustrations show several samples of noisy and quiet things, including a game to play that is quiet and instruments to make that are noisy. (1-2)

Opposite Set. **Old and New.** New York: Grosset and Dunlap, 1977.

A good picture book of the opposites old and new. Good illustrations. (1-2)

Poldendorf, Illa. **Things Are Alike and Different.** Chicago: Children's Press, 1970.

A book comparing things that are alike and different. The author looks at shapes, flowers, leaves and animals. (2)

Provenson, Alice, and Provenson, Martin. **Karen's Opposites.** New York: Golden Press, 1963.

A nicely illustrated book of opposites about two little girls. (1-2)

Radlauer, Ruth, and Radlauer, Ed. **Father Is Big.** Los Angeles: Bowmar Pub. Co., 1967.

A little boy compares his size with the size his father. Everything that belongs to Father is bigger. The little boy decides that he wants to be big also. (1-2)

Ramirez, Carolyn. **Small as a Raisin, Big as the World.** New York: Harvey House, Inc., 1961.

The author describes things that are enormous, very big, medium-sized, little and wee-small. (1-2)

Scarry, Richard. **Short and Tall.** New York: Golden Press, 1976.

This book uses illustrations and stories to tell about these opposites: short/tall, top/bottom, long/short, wide/narrow, big/little, thick/thin, fat/skinny, wet/dry, cold/hot, light/dark, open/closed and polite/rude. (1-2)

Schwartz, Julius. **Uphill and Downhill.** New York: McGraw-Hill Book Co., 1965.

The author tells about the many ways hills can be used and the many different shapes of hills. (2)

Stanek, Muriel. **Left, Right, Left, Right!** Chicago: Albert Whitman and Co., 1976.

Poor Katie has trouble remembering which is left and which is right. Her grandmother gives her a special ring to put on her right hand to remind her which is which. (1-2)

Stiles, Norman, and Wilcox, Daniel. **Grover and the Everything in the Whole Wide World Museum.** New York: Random House, 1974.

Grover visits the Everything in the Whole Wide World Museum and uses these concept words: up, down, under, long, thin, tall, light and heavy. (1-2)

Webber, Irma E. **Up Above and Down Below.** New York: William R. Scott, Inc., no date.

The concepts "up above" and "down below" are explored in this book. The book uses illustrations to show that there are animals that live below the ground as well as above the ground. In the same illustrations, there are plants that live below and above the ground. (2)

Youldon, Gilliam. **Sizes.** London: Franklin Watts, 1979.

This picture book of words features things that are big and little. (1-2)

Activities

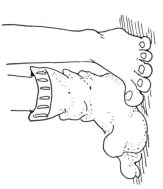

1. While your child is getting dressed or undressed, talk about the concepts of left and right, front and back and over and under. (For example, tell your child to put on the right sock, or to show you the back of the shirt.)

2. Tell your child to pretend he or she is a mouse looking for a new home. Take a walk with your child through your house, and ask your child to tell you all the places a mouse could hide. (One could hide **under** the sink, **above** the living room ceiling, **behind** the wall, etc.)

Take-Me-Home
LEARNING
BOOKLET

Dear Parents,

The concept of opposites is an essential one for your child to understand. Knowing the meaning of words like left, right, down, up, top, bottom, same, different, etc., aids your child in following directions, finding things and in other practical, day-to-day ways.

To make sure that your child really understands these important concepts, please look through the activities and books listed in this booklet. Share several of them with your child. Encourage questions about this subject and practice the concept of opposites as often as possible.

Sincerely,

53

Reading List

Allington, Richard L. **Beginning To Learn About Opposites.** Milwaukee, WI: Raintree Children's Books, 1979.
In this book of opposites, these concept words are illustrated: big/little, same/different, young/old, top/bottom, strong/weak, many/few, front/back, tall/short, alive/dead, left/right, high/low, before/after, far/near and over/under. (1-2)

Berenstain, Stan, and Berenstain, Jan. **Inside, Outside, Upside Down.** New York: Random House, 1968.
Little Bear is inside a box, outside a box and then upside down all the way to town. Good for learning what inside, outside and upside down mean. (K-2)

Eastman, P.D. **Big Dog . . . Little Dog: A Bedtime Story.** New York: Random House, 1973.
A big dog, Fred, and his little dog friend, Ted, like to do the opposite of each other. One likes to ski; one likes to skate. One likes to drive slowly, and the other likes to drive fast. A good story for learning about opposites. (1-2)

3. Make a list of several sets of opposites, and ask your child to play an "Opposites" game with you. You say a word from your list, and your child must tell you the opposite word that goes with it. Talk about the opposites and what they mean.

4. Play "Simon Says" with your child. Be sure to use the concepts left/right, up/down and back/front in the game.

54

Stanek, Muriel. **Left, Right, Left, Right!** Chicago: Albert Whitman and Co., 1976.
Poor Katie has trouble remembering which is left and which is right. Her grandmother gives her a special ring to put on her right hand to remind her which is which. (1-2)

Stiles, Norman, and Wilcox, Daniel. **Grover and the Everything in the Whole Wide World Museum.** New York: Random House, 1974.
Grover visits the Everything in the Whole Wide World Museum and uses these concept words: up, down, under, long, thin, tall, light and heavy. (1-2)

Hann, Jacquie. **Up Day, Down Day.** New York: Four Winds Press, 1978.
A little boy and his friend go fishing together. One of the children catches a cold and must stay home, while the other one has to go to school. Attractive illustrations. (1-2)

Hoban, Tana. **Over, Under and Through.** New York: The Macmillan Co., 1973.
This is a picture book of these concept words: over, under, through, on, in, around, across, between, beside, below, against and behind. Good illustrations. (P-2)

Hughes, Shirley. **Up and Up.** Englewood Cliffs, NJ: Prentice-Hall Inc., 1979.
A picture book about a little girl who eats a very large Easter egg. She is so full that she floats around the sky. Her family tries to get her down using several different methods. (1-2)

Opposite Set. **Big and Little.** New York: Grosset and Dunlap, 1977.
This book is about the opposites big and little, and gives many examples of these concept words. The end of the book has two art ideas and a game that deals with these concepts. (1-2)

Radlauer, Ruth, and Radlauer, Ed. **Father Is Big.** Los Angeles: Bowmar Pub. Co., 1967.
A little boy compares his size with the size his father. Everything that belongs to Father is bigger. The little boy decides that he wants to be big also. (1-2)

NUMBERS

NUMBERS

The concept of numbers, the ability to recognize numerals and the development of the vocabulary of number words, are tools that students use daily. The practical applications of this knowledge are unlimited, and include things like knowing and being able to read addresses and phone numbers, finding a given page in a book, numbering a test paper, telling time, etc. A sound understanding of numbers, numerals and number words is something every student must have.

Many students enter school with the ability to count orally from one to ten. It often happens, however, that they do not recognize the different numerals that stand for these numbers, nor do they recognize the number words when written. Therefore, the activities and books presented in this section deal with the learning and reinforcement of these important number concepts.

Activities

- Divide a piece of paper into one-inch squares. Ask a student to begin in the top left square and write the numerals from 1 on. (Be sure the student numbers from left to right.)

- Make a set of number flashcards using 40 cards. Write one numeral from 1-20 on each of half the cards. Write one number word from one to twenty on each of half the cards. Mix up the cards, and ask a student to match each numeral with its number word. (As a variation, direct a student to put the two sets of cards in order.)

- Select two students to play "Number Match" with the set of cards from the preceding activity. Place all cards face down on a playing surface, and direct the students to take turns turning two cards face up. If the two cards are a numeral and its matching number word, the student keeps that pair and continues. If the two cards do not match, the student returns them to their original positions and the next student takes a turn. When all cards have been matched, the student with more pairs is the winner.

- Help your students make "Number Books." Give each student ten sheets of paper. Direct each student to write one numeral and its corresponding number word on each sheet. Provide magazines from which students may cut out pictures. Tell students to cut out pictures, and paste on each page the same amount of pictures that that number shows (for example, five pictures on the "5" page, seven pictures on the "7" page, etc.).

  This activity may also be done as a whole-class project. After the booklet is completed, add a cover and place it in the classroom library for reference.

- Provide number stencils for students to trace on sandpaper. Direct students to cut out the traced numerals, and glue each to a piece of construction paper. Staple the pages together to make a number booklet for each student. Allow students to illustrate their books, and to take them home for reference.

- Ask a student to make the numerals 1 through 10 (or 20) using clay. After the student has finished, ask him or her to name the numerals as you point to them in random order.

- Check your local library for books of counting rhymes. Find several of these rhymes and teach them to your students. Some of the counting rhymes would be fun for students to pantomime. Try it with the old favorite, "One, two, buckle my shoe . . ."

Allen, Robert. **Numbers: A First Counting Book.** New York: Platt and Munk, 1968.

A book of counting with illustrations of the numerals 1-10. (1-2)

Allington, Richard L. **Beginning To Learn About Numbers.** Milwaukee, WI: Raintree Children's Books, 1979.

A beginning counting book. The author pictures items to count and asks the reader to count each of them. (K-1)

Bradbury, Lynn. **Counting.** Loughborough, England: Ladybird Books, no date.

This book presents illustrations of objects which the reader must count to determine how many are on a page. Good beginning book. (1-2)

Bradbury, Lynn. **Telling the Time.** Loughborough, England: Ladybird Books, no date.

The book illustrates what several people are doing during each hour of the day. (K-2)

Children's Television Workshop. **The Sesame Street Book of Numbers.** New York: Little, Brown, and Co., 1970.

A picture book of the numerals 1-10. (K-2)

Chwast, Seymore and Moskof, Martin. **Still Another Number Book.** New York: McGraw-Hill Book Co., no date.

This is a picture book of addition. The book shows an animal on one page and asks the reader to add it to other animals on the facing page. (1-2)

Federico, Helen. **A Golden Sturdy Book of Counting.** New York: Golden Press, 1971.

This book is made of heavy cardboard for small children. The child must find the items listed on the first page in the picture on the facing page. (P-2)

Hutchins, Pat. **Clocks and More Clocks.** New York: The Macmillan Co., 1970.

A story about a man who bought a clock. He wasn't sure the clock had the correct time, so he bought another one to see if the time was the same. Read more about his adventures. (1-2)

Kennel, Moritz. **Animal Counting Book.** Racine, WI: Golden Press, 1974.

A rhyming book of numbers to be used to introduce counting from 1-10. (1-2)

Klein, Leonard. **Just a Minute.** New York: Harvey House Inc., 1969.

This book explains the following terms: a second, a minute, an hour and twenty-four hours. Good for older children. (2-4)

Kredenser, Gail, and Mack, Stanley. **One Dancing Drum.** New York: S.G. Phillips, 1971.

A number book of band instruments. The author includes the numeral, number word and an example of that number. (1-2)

LeSieg, Theo. **Ten Apples Up On Top.** New York: Random House, 1961.

A lion, a dog and a tiger have an argument about which of them can juggle the most apples. Then a family of bears begins to chase them and they all run into each other and all the apples go flying into the air. What happens when the crash is over? (1-2)

Martin, Bill. **Sounds of Numbers.** New York: Holt, Rinehart and Winston, Inc., 1972.

This book has several rhymes, number stories and stories for reading. (1-2)

The Numbers Book. Newark, NJ: Britannica Discovery Library, 1974.

This numbers book begins with counting, then presents the reader with story problems throughout the remainder of the book. (1-2)

Pierce, Robert, **A Sesame Street Pop-Up: The Counting Book.** Japan: Random House, no date.

This is a pop-up picture book illustrating the numerals 1-10. (K-2)

Scarry Richard. **Learn To Count.** New York: Golden Press, 1976.

Illustrations and poems about the numerals 1-12. (K-2)

Steiner, Charlotte. **10 in a Family.** New York: Alfred A. Knopf, 1960.

A story of two mice that marry and have nine babies. It's a math book as well as a story book; as each baby is born, the author presents an addition problem for the reader. (1-2)

Ungerer, Tomi. **One, Two Where's My Shoe?** New York: Harper and Row, 1964.

In this picture book, a little boy says, "One, two, where's my shoe?" and imagines his shoe in all sorts of weird places. (P-2)

Vogel, Ilse-Margret. **1 2 3, Juggle With Me!** Racine, WI: Golden Press, 1972.

Each animal tries to outdo the others by juggling more balls than the animal preceding it. Finally, the clown teaches them that if they all play together, they can juggle ten balls. (K-2)

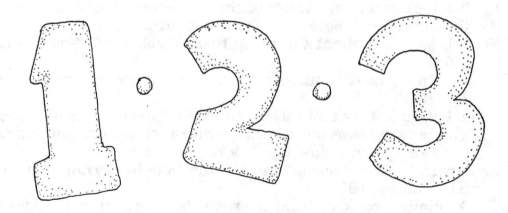

Activities

1. When you and your child are traveling, count all the signs along the way. If your child can recognize numerals, play a number game as you watch the signs. Ask your child to start with the numeral 1, and look for each consecutive number on the signs you see.

2. Have your child count aloud in various ways. Count each piece of clothing as it is put on (or taken off), count pieces to a game, building blocks, doors, chairs, plates, forks — anything that holds your child's interest.

Take-Me-Home LEARNING BOOKLET

Dear Parents,

Understanding numbers is a very important part of learning. Your child needs to be able to say the numbers from one to ten in order. He or she must also understand what each numeral means, and be able to recognize the number word that goes with each numeral.

Right now, we are working at school to make sure your child knows and understands all these things. Please look through the activities and reading list in this booklet, and choose some of these to share with your child at home. This "teamwork" will show your child that you, too, care about learning, and will make numbers a more interesting subject to study.

Sincerely,

Connect the dots to find the secret message.

YOU ARE A

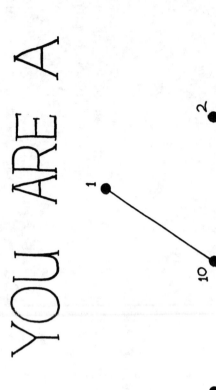

3
2
4
5
1
6
10
8
9
7

---

3. Give your child a "grown-up" book or magazine, and show him or her where the page numbers are to be found. Then call out a page number, and ask your child to turn to that page in the book. Check the page to make sure your child has chosen the right number.

4. Write number words randomly on a sheet of paper. Point to one number word, and ask your child to bring you that many of some object. (For example, point to the word "five," and ask your child to bring you "that many" marbles, spoons, dolls, or whatever.) When your child brings the objects to you, count them together.

Reading List

Allen, Robert. **Numbers: A First Counting Book.** New York: Platt and Munk, 1968.
A book of counting with illustrations of the numerals 1-10. (1-2)

Allington, Richard L. **Beginning To Learn About Numbers.** Milwaukee, WI: Raintree Children's Books, 1979.
A beginning counting book. The author pictures items to count and asks the reader to count each of them. (K-1)

Bradbury, Lynn. **Counting.** Loughborough, England: Ladybird Books, no date.
This book presents illustrations of objects which the reader must count to determine how many are on a page. Good beginning book. (1-2)

Chwast, Seymore and Moskof, Martin. **Still Another Number Book.** New York: McGraw-Hill Book Co., no date.
This is a picture book of addition. The book shows an animal on one page and asks the reader to add it to other animals on the facing page. (1-2)

Federico, Helen. **A Golden Sturdy Book of Counting.** New York: Golden Press, 1971.
This book is made of heavy cardboard for small children. The child must find the items listed on the first page in the picture on the facing page. (P-2)

Kennel, Moritz. **Animal Counting Book.** Racine, WI: Golden Press, 1974.
A rhyming book of numbers to be used to introduce counting from 1-10. (1-2)

Kredenser, Gail, and Mack, Stanley. **One Dancing Drum.** New York: S.G. Phillips, 1971.
A number book of band instruments. The author includes the numeral, number word and an example of that number. (1-2)

LeSieg, Theo. **Ten Apples Up On Top.** New York: Random House, 1961.
A lion, a dog and a tiger have an argument about which of them can juggle the most apples. Then a family of bears begins to chase them and they all run into each other and all the apples go flying into the air. What happens when the crash is over? (1-2)

Martin, Bill. **Sounds of Numbers.** New York: Holt, Rinehart and Winston, Inc., 1972.
This book has several rhymes, number stories and stories for reading. (1-2)

Scarry Richard. **Learn To Count.** New York: Golden Press, 1976.
Illustrations and poems about the numerals 1-12. (K-2)

ADDITIONAL READING LISTS

During the early school years, students are presented with many ideas they need to understand. One of the most important of these is time. For students to develop a sense of time, it is necessary for them to grasp the concepts of a day, a week, a month, a year and the seasons. A full understanding of these concepts helps students develop a framework in which to experience and understand our world.

Holidays are also a major part of every student's world. Whether these days are religious or secular, they are times to anticipate, times to celebrate, times to remember. These special days are landmarks in a child's life, and often, students measure the passing of time between them. These days are special experiences. Knowing about and understanding them add a touch of wonder to a child's world, and provide opportunities for all kinds of learning experiences.

This section of **A-B-C, 1-2-3** has been developed for both teachers and parents who want to explore and enjoy these learning concepts and experiences together with a child.

DAYS OF THE WEEK

Baum, Arline, and Baum, Joseph. **One Bright Monday Morning.** New York: Pinwheel Books (Knopf Pantheon), 1973.
This is a valuable book for learning the days of the week. The reader learns not only the days of the week but also how to count to seven. (K-2)

Delton, Judy. **It Happened on Thursday.** Chicago: Albert Whitman and Co., 1978.
Everything good happened to Jamie on Thursdays. Then one Thursday, Jamie's mom became very sick and had to go to the hospital. Everyone was sad because she was extremely ill and they didn't know if she would get well. Then on a Friday night, the doctor called to say that Jamie's mom was going to be okay. Jamie discovered other days could be special too. (K-3)

Lasker, Joel. **Lentil Soup.** Chicago: Albert Whitman and Co., 1977.
A young farmer's wife tries to please her husband by making lentil soup that tastes just as his mother's did. Each day of the week she tries making the soup a different way. She could never quite please him, so by Saturday, she runs from the kitchen in despair. The soup overcooked, and ended up tasting like his mother's! (K-2)

LeSieg, Theo. **Wacky Wednesday.** New York: Random House, Inc., 1974.
This is a story about a child who awakens one Wednesday morning to find everything completely wacky. There are shoes on the wall, children walking around with no legs, turtles in trees, etc. The child finally decides that he better go back to bed because it's been an awfully wacky day. (K-2)

Pearson, Susan. **Monday I Was an Alligator.** Philadelphia: J.B. Lippincott Co., 1979.
Emily's imagination gets her into trouble every day of the week, from Monday when she is an alligator, to Saturday when she changes into a bull. (K-2)

Schnick, Eleanor. **Rainy Sunday.** New York: The Dial Press, 1981.
This "Easy-to-Read" book is about a little girl on a rainy Sunday afternoon. She tells how she feels about everything around her. (K-2)

Schulevitz, Uri. **One Monday Morning.** New York: Charles Scribner's Sons, 1967.
Each day of the week the King, the Queen and the Prince came to visit the little boy, but he was never home. Finally on Sunday, he was at home and the King, the Queen and the Prince brought lots of people with them to visit the little boy. (K-3)

Viorst, Judith. **Alexander and the Terrible, Horrible, No Good, Very Bad Day.** New York: Atheneum, 1979.

Alexander could tell from the moment he woke up that it was going to be an awful day. And sure enough, it was. In fact, it was so bad that Alexander considered leaving his home and going far away. This book allows the reader to see that anyone can have a bad day. (2-3)

MONTHS OF THE YEAR

Delton, Judy. **My Mom Hates Me in January.** Chicago: Albert Whitman and Co., 1977.

Lee Henry can never do anything right in January. His mom says he's too messy, too noisy and always underfoot. If winter doesn't turn to spring soon, she's going to have a nervous breakdown. Finally, Lee Henry and his mom see a robin outside their window and everything seems to get better because spring is just around the corner. (K-3)

Hall, Donald. **Ox-Cart Man.** New York: The Viking Press, 1979.

The family in this book works together from January through December making things that they can use and things that Pa can sell at the market. The family embroiders, taps sap, whittles and raises crops and animals. (K-3)

Jacobs, Leland B. **April Fool!** Champaign, IL: Garrard Publishing Co., 1973.

Everyone has been playing April Fool jokes on Nancy all day. She gets tired of being the fool, so she decides to play a trick on her mother and father. (K-2)

Krahn, Fernando. **April Fools.** New York: E. P. Dutton and Co., Inc., 1974.

Two little boys design a dragon head and place it on a long stick to play April Fools' jokes. It's fun for a while until they get lost in the forest and can't find their way home. They decide that maybe someone will find them if they hold the stick up in the forest. What happens? (K-3)

Provenson, Alice, and Provenson, Martin. **The Year at Maple Hill Farm.** New York: Atheneum, 1978.

Each month is a new experience with all the animals on the farm. The author discusses all the thing animals do during each month. (K-2)

Sendak, Maurice. **Chicken Soup with Rice.** New York: Harper and Row, 1962.

Each month of the year is good for eating a bowl of chicken soup with rice. In January, eat chicken soup while sliding on the ice and in December, fill the bowl with baubles. Great illustrations. (K-2)

Yolan, Jane. **All in the Woodland Early (An ABC Book).** Cleveland, OH: William Collins Publishing Inc., 1979.

An ABC book about animals out in the woods on a bright May day hunting for friends to play with. (K-3)

 **SEASONS**

Adelson, Leone. **All Ready for Winter.** New York: David McKay Co., Inc., 1952.

A small child compares his preparation for winter with that of the animals. He imagines what it would be like if he swam to the bottom of a pond and dug down deep like the turtle or curled up in a mousehole to go to sleep. The child helps his mother "dig out" his winter things, so he is "All Ready for Winter." (1-3)

Carrick, Carol, and Carrick, Donald. **Swamp Spring.** New York: The Macmillan Co., 1969.

New life begins on a warm spring day. The animals wake up and leave their winter homes to look for new sources of food and lodging. (K-3)

Fox, Charles Philip. **When Autumn Comes.** Chicago: Reilly and Lee Co., 1966.

Preparations for winter are taking place in this book about autumn. The animals prepare their homes for a hard winter as the leaves on the trees turn golden brown and fall to the ground. (K-3)

Fox, Charles Philip. **When Spring Comes.** Chicago: Reilly and Lee Co., 1964.

This is a book about different animals having babies in the spring and how their babies grow. Spring is a time when all things grow, plants as well as animal babies. (1-3)

Fox, Charles Philip. **When Summer Comes.** Chicago: Reilly and Lee Co., 1966.

This book is made up of black-and-white photographs that show mother animals bringing out their babies on a sunny summer day. (K-3)

Fox, Charles Philip. **When Winter Comes.** Chicago: Reilly and Lee Co., 1962.

The black-and-white photographs in this book show animals in their preparations for winter. They must find dry, warm places in which to sleep and enough food to last them all winter. (1-3)

Hoban, Lillian. **Turtle Spring.** New York: Greenwillow Books, 1978.

The turtle children find a bump in the garden and can't figure out what it is. Someone suggests that it's a bomb. This rumor spreads until one little girl turtle discovers that it's a new batch of turtle eggs. (K-2)

Holl, Adelaide. **Bedtime for Bears.** Champaign, IL: Garrard Publishing Co., 1973.

Little Bear does not want to go to bed even though it is getting very cold outside. Mother Bear gives him one last chance to look around before he goes to sleep, but all of his friends are asleep for the winter so he can't visit with them. Mother Bear then puts Little Bear to bed and he falls fast asleep. (P-2)

Miles, Betty. **A Day of Autumn.** New York: Alfred A. Knopf, 1967.
All of the different sights, sounds and smells of autumn are discussed in "A Day of Autumn." (K-2)

Parker, Bertha Morris. **The Wonders of the Seasons.** Racine, WI: Golden Press, 1966.
The seasons are depicted in the colorful pages of this book. Each season is illustrated by the sights, sounds and smells of that time. (K-2)

Scarry, Richard. **All Year Long.** Racine, WI: Golden Press, 1976.
A Richard Scarry book about days of the week, months of the year, seasons, etc. This book is a good introduction to these specific concepts. (K-2)

Yano, Shigeko. **One Spring Day.** Valley Forge, PA: Judson Press, 1977.
In this book of lovely watercolor illustrations depicting a fresh spring day, a young child discovers the wonderment of spring. (K-3)

 # HALLOWEEN

Ahlberg, Janet, and Ahlberg, Allan. **Funnybones.** New York: Greenwillow Books, 1980.
Big skeleton, little skeleton and dog skeleton live in a dark, dark house in a dark, dark cellar. They go out looking for someone to scare and can't find anyone to frighten. They decide to scare each other, and they do. (K-2)

Alexander, Sue. **Witch, Goblin, and Ghost in the Haunted Wood.** New York: Pantheon Books, 1981.
A collection of stories about Witch, Goblin and Ghost and the adventures they share as friends. (K-3)

Benarde, Anita. **The Pumpkin Smasher.** Middletown, CT: Xerox Education Publications, 1972.
Someone was secretly smashing the pumpkins in Cranberry, and the townspeople could never catch the culprit. So, the Turner twins decided to try to solve the mystery. They took a big boulder, painted it orange like a pumpkin and put it in front of the town hall. Do they catch the culprit? (K-3)

Berenstain, Stan, and Berenstain, Jan. **Bears in the Night.** New York: Random House, 1971.
When the bears go exploring in the middle of the night, they become scared out of their wits and run home as quickly as their little legs will carry them. (K-1)

Berenstain, Stan, and Berenstain, Jan. **The Berenstain Bears and the Spooky Old Tree.** New York: Random House, Inc., 1978.
Late one night, three little bears go out on an adventure. Do they dare climb up twisty old stairs, go through moving walls and climb over sleeping big bears? Do the three little bears make it home? (K-2)

Bright, Robert. **Georgie's Halloween.** New York: Doubleday and Co., Inc., 1958.

Halloween is always a special time of year for Georgie the Ghost. This year, the village has a contest for the best costume and Georgie is sure he will win. Does he? (K-2)

Carroll, Ruth. **The Witch Kitten.** Middletown, CT: Weekly Reader Books, 1973.

A picture book about a witch's kitten and the adventures it has when it borrows the witch's broom. (K-2)

DeLage, Ida. **ABC Witch.** Champaign, IL: Garrard Publishing Co., 1977.

The ABC Witch zooms off into the Halloween night, flying from A to Z. This book introduces the ABC's in a Halloween story. (K-2)

Devlin, Wende, and Devlin, Harry. **Old Witch Rescues Halloween.** Pleasantville, NY: Reader's Digest Services, Inc., 1972.

Mr. Butterbean was being mean and ornery as usual and wanted to cancel Halloween. All of the townspeople were very upset about this, especially Old Witch and the family she lived with. That night, there was a meeting at the town hall about the problem, and something strange happened. (K-3)

Freeman, Don. **Space Witch.** New York: The Viking Press, 1959.

Tilly Witch decides that she and her pet cat ought to spend Halloween scaring creatures from other planets. She builds a spaceship and takes off for outer space. Tilly and her cat arrive on a strange planet prepared to scare its inhabitants. What happens to Tilly? (K-2)

Freeman, Don. **Tilly Witch.** New York: The Viking Press, Inc., 1969.

Tilly Witch is Halloween queen, but she is too nice to people and always goes around with a smile on her face. She visits a witch doctor who sends her off to finishing school. Does Tilly turn ferocious once more? (K-2)

Gordon, Sharon. **Three Little Witches.** Mahwah, NJ: Troll Associates, 1980.

Wendy and Wanda have their own unique way of traveling at night, but poor Wilma does not. Who will help her with her problem? (K-1)

Hoff, Syd. **Mrs. Switch.** New York: G.P. Putnam's Sons, 1966.

Mrs. Switch is the last witch in the world, and she finds haunting people isn't fun anymore. What happens when she decides to buy a house and live with her cat in a perfectly normal neighborhood? (K-3)

Kraus, Robert. **How Spider Saved Halloween.** New York: Scholastic Book Services, 1973.

Fly, Ladybug and Spider planned to go trick-or-treating on Halloween, but no matter what Spider wore, he couldn't disguise himself. While they were deciding on their costumes, two bullies came by and smashed Ladybug's pumpkin. That gave the three friends an idea! Did it turn out to be a nice Halloween after all? (K-2)

CHRISTMAS

Allen, France Charlotte. **The Secret Christmas.** New York: G.P. Putnam's Sons, 1971.

Behind the walls in the Christopher's house lives a family of mice. Every Christmas, the mice come out after the Christophers go to bed and collect things for their own Christmas celebration. When Rarebit goes out, he is so overwhelmed by the scene that he is caught by the cat and can't get back to his home. (K-2)

Balian, Lorna. **Bah! Humbug?** Nashville, TN: Abingdon, 1977.

Margie loves Santa and believes in him, but her big brother Arthur says that Santa is just a big, fat humbug. In order to prove his theory, Arthur sets out to trap Santa on Christmas Eve. What happens? (K-2)

Bonsall, Crosby. **Twelve Bells for Santa.** New York: Harper and Row Publishers, 1977.

All of the neighborhood children have a Christmas party and decide that the person with the best Santa costume will win a prize. But who would have suspected that the real Santa would show up? Santa leaves the party before the children can give him his prize. What will the children do? (K-2)

Carrisk, Carol. **Paul's Christmas Birthday.** New York: Greenwillow Books, 1978.

December 24th, what a day for Paul's birthday. Everyone else is thinking about Christmas. Paul is very upset until his mother tells him that he is going to have a special party with a visitor from outer space. Will Paul have a happy birthday after all? (K-2)

Coopersmiths, Jerome. **A Chanukah Fable for Christmas.** New York: G.P. Putnam's Sons, 1969.

A little Jewish boy dreams about presents, trees and stockings on Christmas. As he is dreaming, who should appear but a man dressed in red! What happens next? (K-3)

De Paola, Tomie. **The Friendly Beasts: An Old Christmas Carol.** New York: G.P. Putnam's Sons, 1981.

This old carol tells of the special roles played by the animals of Bethlehem on the first Christmas Eve.

Hillert, Margaret. **Merry Christmas, Dear Dragon.** Chicago: Follett Publishing Co., 1981.

This is a "Just Beginning To Read Book" about a boy and a dragon who become friends and spend Christmas together. (K-1)

Hoban, Lillian. **Arthur's Christmas Cookies.** New York: Harper and Row Publishers, 1972.

Arthur's presents always turn out wrong. He wants this Christmas to be different. He decides to make Christmas cookies for his mother and father, but the cookies turn out to be very salty and hard. What can Arthur do with the cookies to make things turn out all right? (K-3)

Hoff, Syd. **Merry Christmas, Henrietta.** Champaign, IL: Garrard Publishing Co., 1980.

Henrietta wants to buy a special Christmas gift for Mr. Gray because he has been so good to all the farm animals. She goes into town to ask Santa for his advice. Surprisingly, Santa asks a favor of Henrietta. How are these Christmas problems solved? (K-2)

Knight, Hilary. **The Twelve Days of Christmas.** New York: The Macmillan Co., Inc., 1981.

Benjamin Bear brings Bedelia a surprise on each of the twelve days before Christmas. The beautiful illustrations are completed in great detail. (K-3)

Krahn, Fernando. **The Biggest Christmas Tree on Earth.** Boston: Little Brown and Co., 1978.

While wandering through the forest, a little girl discovers a group of animals decorating a large pine tree. She hurries back into town to lead the villagers to the scene. (K-2)

Mendoza, George. **The Christmas Tree Alphabet Book.** New York: The World Publishing Co., 1971.

In this Christmas ABC book, children throughout the world prepare something special for Christmas. (K-3)

Miller, Edna. **Mousekin's Christmas Eve.** Englewood Cliffs, NJ: Prentice-Hall, Inc., 1965.

Mousekin's human family has moved out of the house. The little creature wanders about in the cold, snowy night searching for warmth and stray crumbs to nibble. At last, he discovers lights, music and laughter coming from another house. He enters into a new world of warmth, love and peacefulness.

Moncure, Jane Belk. **Our Christmas Book.** Elgin, IL: The Child's World, 1977.

Miss Berry's third grade class prepares for Christmas by doing art projects, singing Christmas songs, making toys for a toy parade and setting up a display of Christmas items from around the world. This book features exciting art projects for children to make. (K-3)

Schick, Alice, and Schick, Joel. **Santaberry and the Snard.** Philadelphia, PA: J.P. Lippincott Co., 1976.

Santa's elves insisted that there were Snards living in the area, but Santa would not believe them. Then, on the night before Christmas Eve, Santa was gobbled up by a Snard! Mrs. Claus was frantic because it was almost time for Santa to load his sleigh and be on his way. How do Santa and the Snard come to terms in time to salvage Christmas? (K-3)

Schick, Joel. **Joel Schick's Christmas Present.** Philadelphia, PA: J.B. Lippincott Co., 1977

In this offbeat version of "The Twelve Days of Christmas," monsters are depicted throughout the book rather than the traditional people and animals. The illustrations are appealing to children. (K-2)

VALENTINE'S DAY

Adams, Adrienne. **The Great Valentine's Day Balloon Race.** New York: Charles Scribner's Sons, 1980.

Orson and Bonnie Bunny wanted to enter the big hot-air balloon contest on Valentine's Day. Their mother and father helped them build a balloon and test it so that it would be ready for the big day. Do Orson and Bonnie win the contest? (K-3)

Balian, Lorna. **A Sweetheart for Valentine.** Nashville, TN: Abingdon, 1979.

One morning, the people of St. Valentine village discovered a large basket on the steps of the town hall. Inside was a very large baby. She was such a large baby that the villagers decided to take care of her as a group. They named the child Valentine. What happened to Valentine as she grew up? (K-3)

Brown, Marc. **Arthur's Valentines.** Boston: Little Brown and Co., 1980.

Arthur's secret admirer kept sending him valentines, but Arthur couldn't figure out who his admirer was. Each day of the week he received a new love note. Solve this Valentine mystery with Arthur! (K-2)

Bulla, Clyde Robert. **St. Valentine's Day.** New York: Thomas Y. Crowell Co., 1965.

This book follows the history of St. Valentine's Day from its inception during early Roman times until the present. Learn about this holiday and how its traditions and customs have been passed from one generation to the next. (2-6)

Cohen, Miriam. **"Bee My Valentine."** New York: Greenwillow Books, 1978.

Jim was excited because Valentine's Day was coming. He liked getting cards from his friends, and he enjoyed giving them, too. But this year, Jim did not receive many valentines, and he felt very sad. What could happen to make Jim feel better? (K-2)

De Paola, Tomie. **Things To Make and Do for Valentine's Day.** New York: Franklin Watts, 1976.

This is a book of things to make for Valentine's Day. Some of the activities include making paint-printed cards, envelopes, valentine mailbags, a heart tree, bakers' clay objects and holiday sandwiches and desserts. (K-6)

Schulz, Charles M. **Be My Valentine Charlie Brown.** New York: Scholastic Book Services, 1976.

Miss Othmar's class was having a Valentine's party. All of the children had planned special valentines for their girlfriends or boyfriends. Poor Charlie Brown didn't receive any valentine cards. He felt neglected and rejected. Did his friends make it up to him? (1-3)

EASTER

Adams, Adrienne. **The Easter Egg Artists.** New York: Charles Scribner's Sons, 1976.

The Abbotts are designers of Easter eggs who also happen to be rabbits. They are worried about their son, Orson, and what his plans for the future are. But after noticing that he always completes each project he starts, they realize that there is no need to worry because Orson is going to turn out to be a good Easter bunny. (K-3)

Carrick, Carol. **A Rabbit for Easter.** New York: Greenwillow Books, 1979.

Sam's kindergarten class has a rabbit for a pet, and Sam is selected to take care of it over Easter vacation. He does a fine job until one day he cannot find the bunny. What will he tell the other children? (K-2)

Kroll, Steven. **The Big Bunny and the Easter Egg.** New York: Holiday House, 1983.

Wilbur is a very special Easter bunny because he is strong enough to carry lots of baskets and he always delivers the Easter goodies on time. This Easter he has everything ready, but he becomes very ill. Will his friends rally to help deliver the goodies? (K-3)

Moncure, Jane Belk. **Our Easter Book.** Elgin, IL: The Child's World, 1976.

Miss Berry and her third grade class decorate their classroom for Easter. They make flowers and puppets, sing songs, decorate a tree and dye eggs. They also go to a petting zoo where they are allowed to pet the baby animals. (K-3)

Schulz, Charles M. **It's the Easter Beagle, Charlie Brown.** New York: Scholastic Book Services, 1976.

Charlie Brown and his friends are at it again. Their plans are underway for Easter, but Linus keeps insisting that the Easter Beagle will take care of everything. Is Snoopy really the Easter Beagle? (1-3)

Wahl, Jan. **Old Hippo's Easter Egg.** New York: Harcourt Brace Jovanovich, 1980.

Old Hippo dreams of having a child that he can teach, tend and love. One Easter morning, Old Hippo and Pocket Mouse find an egg in a basket on their front doorstep. They ask their friend Auntie Sheep to hatch it for them. When a tiny duckling emerges from the egg, Old Hippo's dream comes true. What happens when the season changes and the duckling must fly south. (K-3)

Weil, Lisl. **The Candy Egg Bunny.** New York: Holiday House, 1975.

This is an interpretation of how Easter bunnies first began delivering candy eggs to boys and girls all over the world. Walter does not believe in the Easter bunnies until one hops right up to him and tells him the story. (K-3)

OTHER SPECIAL DAYS

Aliki. **New Year's Day.** New York: Thomas Y. Crowell Co., 1967.
This book tells the story of the first New Year's Day when the Romans created a new calendar designating January as the first month of the year. It also explores the celebration of New Year's Day all over the world. (1-6)

Balian, Lorna. **Leprachauns Never Lie.** Nashville, TN: Abingdon, 1980.
Ninny Nanny sits around all day and does nothing to help take care of her sick grandmother. Then one day, she finds a leprachaun and thinks that he will give her his pot of gold. Does he? (K-3)

Balian, Lorna. **Sometimes It's Turkey — Sometimes It's Feathers.** Nashville, TN: Abingdon Press, 1973.
Mrs. Grimm finds an egg in the forest. She takes it home and cares for it until a turkey hatches from it. She feeds the little chick, thinking that the turkey will be a tasty Thanksgiving dinner. But after taking care of it from April through November, will she really use the hatchet? (K-3)

Carle, Eric. **The Secret Birthday Message.** New York: Thomas Y. Crowell, 1971.
A secret message has been sent to Tim on the night before his birthday. He must break the code in order to find his birthday present. Will he decipher the code and find his gift? (K-3)

Delton, Judy. **Groundhog's Day at the Doctor.** New York: Parents Magazine Press, 1981.
Groundhog woke up feeling not quite himself. He ached and felt stiff, so he went to see the doctor. While waiting for the doctor, Groundhog helped every patient that walked in. When the doctor was finally ready to see patients, there were none! What advice do you think the doctor gave Groundhog? (K-3)

Evenson, A. E. **About the History of the Calendar.** Chicago: Children's Press, 1972.
This book of calendars traces the development of the days, weeks, months and years we live by. (3-6)

Fisher, Aileen. **Arbor Day.** New York: Thomas Y. Crowell Co., 1965.
This book is about trees and soil and how to conserve these wonderful gifts. The author talks about a man named J. Sterling Morton who felt that there should be a special day to honor these treasures. Read this book to learn about the history of Arbor Day. (2-6)

McGovern, Ann. **The Pilgrim's First Thanksgiving.** New York: Scholastic Book Services, 1973.
This story of the Pilgrims begins with their decision to leave England and takes the reader through their first Thanksgiving feast in the New World. (K-3)

McGovern, Ann. **Why It's a Holiday.** New York: Random House, 1960.
This resource book of special days and holidays on a primary grade level includes New Year's Day, Memorial Day, Thanksgiving and many others. (2-3)

Moncure, Jane Belk. **Our Mother's Day Book.** Elgin, IL: The Child's World, 1977.

Celebrating and preparing for Mother's Day can be exciting, especially if you're in Miss Berry's third grade class. The children discuss Mother's Day and how it's celebrated around the world. (K-3)

Purcell, John Wallace. **The True Book of Holidays and Special Days.** Chicago: Children's Press, 1955.

The author has included holidays from Columbus Day to Christmas to the Fourth of July in a format that young children in second and third grade can understand. (2-3)

Rockwell, Ann, and Rockwell, Harlow. **Happy Birthday To Me.** New York: The Macmillan Co., Inc., 1981.

Preparations for a birthday party are underway. The child in the story tells how he gets ready for his special day. He has a wonderful day with all of his friends. (K-3)

Schertle, Alice. **The April Fool.** New York: Lee and Shepard Books, 1981.

The King is unhappy because his feet hurt all the time. His subjects make him angry, and his prime minister has to carry him everywhere because of his aching feet. Each month a different Fool attempts to amuse the King. In April, he hires a new Fool who tells him he will find the most comfortable shoes in the world for the King. This is the story of how he does just that. (K-3)

Scott, Geoffrey. **Labor Day.** Minneapolis, MN: Carolrhoda Books, 1982.

This book tells how Labor Day became a holiday in the United States. The author explains how the holiday honors all American workers, and how labor unions got started in the United States. (2-4)

Showers, Paul. **Columbus Day.** New York: Thomas Y. Crowell Co., 1965.

This is the story of Columbus and how he discovered America. The book tells how we celebrate this very special day in October. (1-6)

Tina, Dorothy Les. **Flag Day.** New York: Thomas Y. Crowell Co., 1965.

On June 14, 1877, Congress asked that the American flag be flown from all public buildings. In 1885, a teacher had his class celebrate the flag's birthday. This book tells about our flag's history and the events that led up to the declaration of this holiday. (1-6)

Williams, Barbara. **Chester Chipmunk's Thanksgiving.** New York: E. P. Dutton, 1978.

Chester Chipmunk wants to share his Thanksgiving dinner with his cousin Archie, but Archie is not feeling well and will not come over. Chester invites other friends, but they can't come either. Finally, Chester talks Oswald Opossum into sharing Thanksgiving with him. Just as Chester and Oswald are ready to eat, something exciting happens. (K-2)